# Groundwork Essentials

## Foundation that Lasts a Lifetime

### Kim Baker

# DEDICATION

To Janice and Brad, for teaching me groundwork is the key to a great relationship with your horse and everything you know about how to start horses and help troubled horses and their people improve their relationship.

To The Horses - The Master Teachers
I learn something new from each one of you.

Thank you!

# CONTENTS

# ACKNOWLEDGMENTS

I would like to thank Lisette Zandvoort for taking all of the photographs for this book. I would like to thank Bernadette and John at Happy Dog Ranch for allowing me to work with WindTalker. I would like to thank Kathleen June for allowing Qamar to be showcased in this book. Thanks to Ellen Haight, my wonderfully talented editor. Thanks to all the wonderful horsemen and women who have taught and inspired me along the way.

# DISCLAIMER OF LIABILITY

# 1 INTRODUCTION

Nothing we do with horses is truly natural to them. Building trust, gaining respect and establishing leadership with your horse are vital elements in a successful relationship. The following exercises, taught to me by my mentor, I have found to be the most beneficial in establishing a wonderful foundation for your horse to be able to excel in our human world.

As prey animals, horses naturally "go into pressure." In the wild, for example, a zebra being attacked by a lion will push back into the lion waiting for that exact moment when the lion releases the zebra to be able to escape. Our domestic horses are the same, in that they instinctually go into pressure. To survive in our human world of tack and horse trailers, a horse must simply understand how to give to pressure. If a horse does not give to pressure, all sorts of bad experiences happen that can traumatize the horse.

The seven exercises described here create a foundation on which you can build a horse's development. I use them when starting colts, and they are useful as tune-up exercises for a horse of any age who needs some assistance, or what some people might call an attitude adjustment. Does your horse not respect your space and walk all over you? Does your horse ignore your cues? These exercises will help you resolve some of the most challenging behavioral problems.

Before starting with these exercises, ensure your horse is healthy and fit to do the work you are asking him to do. These exercises help you establish a baseline for what is normal for your horse and you'll be able to see very quickly if your horse is not performing to normal standards, and/or your horse is stiff somewhere in his body.

## Equipment
I use the Buck Brannamen Collection (halter and lead rope) by Double Diamond. I use a 12 or 14 foot lead rope with no metal clasp. Twelve feet is the minimum length of lead rope you should use for these exercises. Ensure your halter fits your horse properly. A halter that

is too tight can cause nerve damage in only 10-20 seconds. You should be able to get at least two to three fingers in between your horse's face and the halter. Position the nose band knots just below the facial crest bone on either side of your horse's "cheeks."

The reason I like Buck's Collection is because the halter is soft, provides clear communication to the horse and is more similar to a bridle than other rope halter styles, and there is no metal clasp attaching the lead rope to the halter. If you need to send a lot of energy down the lead rope to get your horse's attention I do not want the metal clasp hitting the chin and jaw bones.

Nose band knots are below WindTalker's facial crest bones (the facial crest bone is just above the knuckles of my left hand). I can get several fingers between his face and the halter, so it is not too tight. You can see the halter is made of soft yacht type rope and there is no metal clasp attaching the lead rope to the halter. I am using a twelve foot length lead rope.

*Note: In this book I refer to the horse as "he" or "him." This is not to discredit or omit mares, it is for the simple ease of clarity in the prose and to lessen confusion in understanding the exercises.*

# 2 STARTING POSITION

With your horse haltered and a lead rope attached, stand facing your horse with your shoulders square to his shoulders. There should be a nice dip in the lead rope with your horse is in his personal space bubble and you in yours. When you need to enter your horse's space, ask for permission by softening your body language and presenting your side, then offer your hand to his nose with your palm facing down. Once your horse acknowledges you, you can step into his space to begin an exercise.

By facing our horse and asking permission to enter into his space, we build trust and respect in our relationship – vital aspects of any healthy relationship. How can we ask our horses to trust and respect us, if we don't return that trust and respect?

I am standing square facing Qamar. There is a nice dip in my lead rope. He is in his personal space bubble and I am in my personal space bubble. This is your starting position for every exercise.

Now I am going to turn my body to the side. I am offering my hand palm facing down, and asking permission to enter WindTalker's space.

WindTalker has acknowledged my request by touching his nose to my palm, and now I enter into his space to start an exercise.

# 3 REPETITION

I was taught to teach horses in threes. Science has found three to be the magic number with horses. Do an exercise three times, then move to the other side and repeat three times on that side. Remember, though, your horse may understand sooner or later than three repetitions. If your horse licks and chews, release on whatever repetition that was and do the other side. You can always come back to an exercise and rework it later during your training session.

As soon as your horse has mastered these exercises, do not keep drilling him on them over and over. After each exercise I explain the significance of the exercise and how you can utilize it in the real world. Many of the exercises are good warm up or cool down exercises. You can also use them in unfamiliar surroundings to help settle your horse's nerves. The key is DO NOT keep your horse in kindergarten by doing only these exercises over and over. He is going to get bored and that could lead to a new set of behavioral issues. Once mastered, use the exercises sparingly and move on to new challenges.

# 4 REWARD

Always reward the slightest try. Your horse is not going to master the exercise the first time or even the fifth time. Each horse is an individual and learns at his own pace. If you always reward the slightest try, you won't push your horse beyond the breaking point. Break the exercises down into smaller steps. I have helped you do that, but in some cases you may need to break it down into even smaller steps, based on what your individual horse needs.

I am rewarding Qamar for a job well done. I am stroking him on his forehead between his eyes. He is accepting this by closing his eyes. If your horse does not like to be touched on the face, then you can stroke his neck as a reward. Slow, soft, smooth strokes is better than patting your horse.

# 5 SOAK TIME

Remember that your horse needs time to process what he is learning. Unlike humans who like to go at warp speed and want everything done yesterday, horses need time to process what they are learning. Giving your horse a moment or two to allow the exercise to sink in (soak time) gets you further along the progress chart than if you just cram everything onto your horse at once. Number One rule in Natural Horsemanship is: "Slow is Fast." Horses need their soak time, so be patient!

I am providing WindTalker his soak time. You can see by his relaxed nature he is processing the work we have just completed. Horses need this time to comprehend what you are teaching them. Do NOT skip this important part of the training process.

# 6 HEAD DROPS

Stand on one side of your horse facing his head. Place one hand over your horse's nose and the other over his poll. Apply steady downward pressure until your horse drops his head (even if he only drops his head one centimeter) and release your hands. Reward your horse so he understands he did what you want. Repeat the exercise a couple more times. When your horse appears to have a good understanding of what you want (it doesn't have to be perfect), repeat the exercise on the other side of your horse's head.

I have entered WindTalker's space and I am standing between his shoulders and his head, facing his head.

I place my hands over the nose and the poll and apply steady downward pressure.

You can see Qamar has lowered his head. I released the pressure as soon as he did, and now I'm asking him to lower his head again.

You can see Qamar released himself from the pressure, as there is a good gap between his head and my hands.  When your horse is understanding this exercise this is what you will see.  The horse releases himself by giving fully into the pressure.

## Troubleshooting

If your horse pushes back into your hands and raises his head, keep your hands in position as much as possible. Even if your horse's head goes beyond your reach, keep your hands raised toward his head until he drops his head even the slightest bit. Always reward the slightest try so your horse understands what you want. If your horse starts to back up, or move his head to either side, go with your horse. Keep your hands raised toward his head if he raises his head beyond your reach and follow your horse. The moment your horse drops his head (even the tiniest amount), release and walk your horse forward and start over.

WindTalker is pushing back into my hands. He is a tall horse and I have to reach pretty far to keep my hand over his poll. If he pushed beyond my reach I would still keep my hands raised until he lowered his head the smallest amount.

## Advanced Head Drops

Stand on the side of your horse's head (between his head and shoulder) and apply steady downward pressure on the lead rope underneath your horse's head. Release the moment your horse lowers his head, even if it's only one centimeter. Reward your horse. Repeat the exercise a couple more times and then go to the other side of your horse and do the exercise on that side.

I apply steady downward pressure on the lead rope.

Qamar gives to the pressure, releasing himself and lowering his head.

You can see the actual downward pressure on the halter and lead rope.

Qamar giving to that pressure.

## Troubleshooting

If your horse pulls back against the lead rope pressure, hold your ground as much as possible. You are not going to win a tug-of-war, but stay focused and apply as much pressure as you can. Even if your horse starts to move around, follow him and apply as much downward pressure as you can. Release the moment he gives to that pressure, then walk your horse forward and start again.

StarFire is resisting against the pressure, just a little. Some horses will really resist and "pull back." If your horse is really resisting, then go back to the beginning head drops and make sure he understands the concept of giving to pressure before you advance to this maneuver.

## Significance

Head drops teach your horse to give to pressure. The pressure can come from being tied, getting tangled or caught in something (e.g., halter catching on a fence post) and your riding cues. If your horse understands how to release himself (i.e., give to pressure) he will be able to avoid bad accidents such as pulling back when tied. He will also lead and load into a horse trailer more easily. In riding, to achieve collection, your horse needs to be able to give to the bridle. All bridles put pressure at the poll. You can also use it as a head lowering cue to help your horse relax when something has frightened him.

# 7 LATERAL FLEXION

Stand at or slightly in front of your horse's withers and put one hand on the halter and one hand on your horse's neck between C1 and C3 vertebrae. With light pressure on the halter ask your horse to give to the pressure by turning his head toward you, bending through his neck. As soon as your horse gives his head toward you, release the pressure from the halter, but do not let go of the halter. Use only your fingers on the halter, not your entire hand gripping the halter as that is a safety hazard and you could lose your hand if your horse spooks and takes off. Continue to ask your horse to bring his head around until his nose reaches his side. Note: a horse with neck vertebrae or the poll out will not be able to reach this far back. Through this exercise you will learn what the normal range is for your horse. When in doubt, consult your veterinarian and chiropractor.

I place my hand between C1 and C3 on the neck, then with my fingertips I apply pressure on the halter to ask WindTalker to bring his head around to me.

You can see the pressure I am applying to the halter. Each time WindTalker gives to the pressure I pause, then ask again and bring his nose around a little bit at a time.

Qamar reaching his head around to his side.

When you release your horse's head you want to "give his head back" to him instead of allowing him to whip his head back around (taking his head back). To encourage your horse to understand you giving his head back, gradually release his head, using pressure on the halter if he tries to take it back. In this motion your horse will feel pressure on the halter as he tries to take his head back and you "bump" him into giving into the pressure and slowly allow him to straighten his neck.

WindTalker is bracing against the pressure.  I just wait for him to give into the pressure.

WindTalker gave to the pressure.

## Advanced Lateral Flexion

Stand behind your horse's withers facing his head. Using the lead rope make a C curve and ask your horse to bring his head around to his side. Your horse should feel like ounces on the lead rope instead of pounds of pressure during this exercise.

I start my C arc curve with the lead rope.

Qamar is pretty light, I don't have a lot of pressure on the lead rope and he is bringing his nose around.

Qamar's nose continues to come around.

We complete the advanced lateral flexion exercise.

## Troubleshooting

If your horse wants to move his feet during this exercise, move with him while you continue trying to bring his head around. The moment he stops moving his feet, release his head and go stand in front of him. Soon your horse will learn not to move his feet during this exercise. Break down the exercise into smaller and smaller steps working toward the bigger picture as your specific horse requires.

WindTalker is starting to move his feet.

I stay with him as he completely moves around.

I stuck with WindTalker while he moved around until he gave, then I released him.

## Significance

Lateral flexion allows you and horse to achieve many advanced maneuvers in riding such as half passes, turnarounds, counter arc circles, counter canters, and, of course, your one rein stops. A one rein stop allows you the rider to stop your "runaway" horse. One rein is more powerful than two, because the horse can brace against the pressure of two reins more easily than he can one rein.

# 8 PUSH ME PULL ME

Stand several feet in front of your horse facing him. Use your personal energy bubble to push against his personal energy bubble. Release as soon as your horse shifts his weight backward or takes one step backward. Repeat until your horse understands your cue and starts to back up. Once your horse is good with one step back, increase to two steps, three steps, etc. Once your horse masters backing up, start to incorporate pulling your horse toward you. After your horse backs, immediately begin to back up yourself and bring your horse forward a couple of steps. Apply pressure on the lead rope to get your horse to move forward, if necessary. When you've backed as far as you want to go, immediately begin to bring your horse forward by backing up yourself. The final product of the exercise is to flow like a couple dancing, moving back and forth. Always end the exercise with bringing your horse forward.

I raise my hand and walk to Qamar pushing my bubble into Qamar's bubble. You can see he is beginning to move backwards.

With a horse that knows this exercise well you can move a large distance back and forward. You can see I never get too close to Qamar, he understands the exercise well.

Now I shift, and I start to move backwards, asking Qamar to follow me.

When I'm done, I just stop and put my hands at my waist. This is the cue to stop.

## Troubleshooting

If your personal energy doesn't work in getting your horse to shift his weight backward, you can use the tail of your lead rope at his chest to help increase your energy. Get as big and "loud" as you need to with the energy to get your point across…soon you won't need as much energy.

I am getting big with my energy. I am more animated than I needed to be with Qamar.

My big energy didn't work, so before I ran into WindTalker I used the tail of my lead rope to tap him on the chest to get him to take a step backwards. Remember in the beginning you do one step at time, starting with just shifting the weight back. The final product will look like Qamar.

If your horse goes sideways instead of backing up straight, you can fix the straightness once your horse understands the exercise; until then don't worry how crookedly he backs. Correct a crooked back by turning your horse's head in the direction of the crookedness. For example, if your horse's hindquarters are backing to the right, then turn your horse's head to the right until he straightens out. Release for one step of backing straight. When your horse is good with one step, then ask for two straight steps, then three, etc. until he's backing straight all the time.

Qamar starts to want to back crooked, and I just redirect his nose with a bump on the lead rope to straighten him out.

Apply steady pressure on the lead rope, if your horse does not readily follow you forward.

## Significance

Push Me Pull Me comes in handy in your day-to-day interactions with your horse. Sometimes your horse gets antsy and creeps into your space. With this exercise you can easily back him up out of your space and reestablish a respectful distance between one another. You can use this exercise when teaching a horse to ground tie - if he understands your energy projection you can help him stay in place. This exercise is also good for leading your horse in and out of gates, in and out of the horse trailer, and in new and unfamiliar places. Once your horse respects your space, you will be able to navigate many obstacles and challenges as they arise with ease, safety, and grace. You'll be the envy of your barn pals.

# 9 DISENGAGE HINDQUARTERS

Stand just behind the withers and ask for lateral flexion. Once your horse is soft in his lateral flexion, turn your body and face his hips. Outwardly project your energy toward his hip. If your horse has not started to move away from you, increase the pressure by swinging the tail of your lead rope at his hind leg closest to you and start to step into his space. The instant your horse fully crosses the hind leg closest to you over the outer hind leg, release all pressure, come out of his space and go stand in front of him. Your timing will be important to not release for a cheater try, but to release for a full cross. A cheater try is anything other than a full cross. Repeat on the same side until you feel your horse understands what you are asking of him. Then go and work on the opposite side of your horse, repeating the steps and release points.

I got lateral flexion first, then I change my body language and turn to face Qamar's hip.

Qamar easily disengages his hindquarters for me. See the full cross of the hind legs.

Since Qamar crossed his hind legs, I release him by stepping out of his space.

We re-establish our respectful space distance as Qamar comes forward to square himself up.

## Troubleshooting

To properly disengage the hindquarters, your horse must have lateral flexion. If your horse is stiff as a board with no lateral flexion, he cannot properly disengage his hindquarters. A proper disengagement is the crossing over of one hind leg over the other. In the beginning some horses will cheat and just barely cross their hind legs. Unless there is a physical reason why the horse cannot cross the hind legs, a full cross is expected.

Note: In the beginning your horse may get confused between lateral flexion and disengage the hindquarters. To clarify which exercise you want, ensure your body language is correct. For lateral flexion stand facing your horse's head. For disengage the hindquarters you turn your body/chest and face toward your horse's hips. As long as you are consistent with this body language, your horse will learn the difference between the two exercises. If your horse starts to move his feet, go with him while you ask for lateral flexion. Once you get lateral flexion, release your horse, go stand in front so your horse understands what you wanted. With time you will be able to wait out your horse's movement, get the lateral flexion, then turn and ask for the disengagement of the hindquarters. Read your horse, and know where he is in the process as you're progressing.

Your intention also plays a role in the exercises, so be clear in your own mind what it is you're asking from your horse. Know which exercise are you asking for from you horse before you step into his space. If you get confused, simply step out of your horse's space, go stand in front, clear your mind and start over. No one is perfect and even we get confused. The great thing about horses is their forgiving nature.

I wait and release WindTalker because he became confused between Lateral Flexion and Disengage Hindquarters.

I offer a little assistance with the lead rope to encourage WindTalker to move away from me.

I stay with him and keep projecting my energy to get WindTalker to move away from me.

Finally WindTalker crosses his hind legs, but it took effort on my part to help him figure out what I wanted.

## Advanced Disengage Hindquarters

Once your horse fully understands the exercise and is consistent in disengaging his hindquarters, you can step up the exercise to a more advanced level. This exercise requires at least three full crosses of the hind legs in a row (as I was taught because the magic number is three). This means that if your horse fully crosses two times in a row, but cheats/misses on the third, then your count of three starts over again with one. It must be at least three full crosses in a row. Once your horse has completed the three full crosses, step out of his space, stand in front of him and reward him for a job well done. This exercise should be done on both sides of your horse. By doing at least three full crosses in a row it helps prepare your horse for even more advanced maneuvers like complete 360 degree turns on the front quarters (the hindquarters move around the front quarters).

In Advanced Disengage Hindquarters, keep moving into your horse's hip to keep your horse moving away from you. Qamar is crossing his hind legs.

I keep moving, and Qamar keeps moving away.

I keep moving, and so does Qamar as he is preparing to cross his hind legs again.

Qamar crosses his hind legs again as we've almost completed a 180 degree circle.

## Significance

Now you have your one rein stop on the ground. A one rein stop is lateral flexion, then disengagement of the hindquarters which shifts your horse into neutral. The actual cross of the hind legs is what shifts your horse into neutral. This will directly apply in the saddle. You ask for lateral flexion first, then disengagement of the hindquarters. This is also a great warm up and cool down exercise for your horse in the future. It's a way to evaluate your horse for the day. Is he feeling ok, is he sore, etc.? If your horse has consistently crossed his hind legs for you and now he cannot do it, something physically has changed and he needs to be evaluated by your veterinarian. You will also be able to detect stiffness in your horse's body with this exercise. Is he stiff in the neck, shoulders, ribs, hindquarters?

Note: A more advanced one rein stop is lifting one rein straight up into the sky and, as your horse slows down, asking for lateral flexion and disengagement of the hindquarters. The one rein straight up into the sky jams your horse in the mouth and starts to lock up his body, preventing the forward movement at a fast pace, enabling you to be able to complete the traditional one rein stop more safely and effectively.

# 10 CIRCLING

Stand facing your horse. "Open a door" in the direction you want your horse to go by raising that arm (right or left) straight out into a T position and ask your horse to move around you. You can use the tail of your lead rope on the outside shoulder to help move your horse off to the side and forward. DO NOT go toward his hindquarters to try to get him to move forward; your horse will then be lunging you. You stand still as if you are on a pitcher's mound and ask the horse to move around you. If the horse backs up try to hold your ground, or ask him to come forward toward you, then ask him to move off on the circle again. With a really resistant horse you may need to follow him backing up then release as soon as he moves sideways. A horse might also move into the pressure you are putting on the outside shoulder (natural instinct). Again hold your ground, continue to increase your pressure until the horse moves away. The moment the horse moves away, reward by releasing the pressure. Pause for a moment, then ask your horse to move out on the circle again by starting the process over. Reward for each little baby step your horse takes out on the circle. As your horse is moving around on the circle, your focus is on his rib cage right where your leg would be if you were riding him. Focus your gaze and your chest on this spot and continue to turn slightly as he moves around you on the circle. To stop, bring your hands together into your belly button and back up until your horse is straight (this is the ONLY time you get off your pitcher's mound). To change directions, drop the tail of the rope and grab the rope in front of your other hand and bring your arms out into a T position. Use your rope tail to help push the new outside shoulder out away from you and direct your horse back out on the circle. Once your horse understands the exercise, you can begin to ask for up and down transitions. Use your personal energy and the tail of the lead rope as your gas pedal for up transitions, and use your breath (deep breath in and let it all out) to bring him down a gait. You can also incorporate voice commands.

I am standing facing Qamar.

I open my left door asking Qamar to move around me to the left.

Qamar continues to move out onto the circle.

Qamar is moving out on the circle going around me, I have relaxed my body language so he maintains his walking gait. I continue to focus my chest on Qamar's rib cage where my leg would be if I were riding him.

I have dropped the tail of my lead rope, and changed my hands on the lead rope in preparation to ask Qamar to change directions. You can see he is responding to the change in my body language.

I continue to open my door in the new direction to help Qamar go the opposite direction.

You can see my door is nice and open, I start to follow up with energy from my right hand on Qamar's outside shoulder to help guide him in the new direction.

I relax my body language as Qamar has completed the change of directions.

Here's another shot of my body language for changing directions.

My body language is for asking for more speed on the circle. Open your door so your horse has somewhere to go with the faster speed.

Once Qamar is trotting I relax my body language again so he mains the trot until I ask him to do something different. When I want to downshift I just take in a deep breath and let it all out and my horse will downshift.

## Troubleshooting

The biggest issue I see with the Circle exercise is people trying to move the horse. You need to stand still as if you were on a pitcher's mound and you cannot come off that pitcher's mound except when you want to stop your horse. When you move off the mound, in essence your horse is moving your feet instead of you moving your horse's feet. The way hierarchy works in the horse herd is by moving other horse's feet. So if you move your feet in an effort to move your horse's feet, you have lost the hierarchy game. Once your horse understands he is to move around, sometimes he will still cut into your personal space. Instead of going out on a nice circle, he cuts off the distance between you and him on his way around you. Hold your ground, use your personal energy bubble just like you did in the Push Me Pull Me exercise. Most likely you will need to step into his space, pushing your energy bubble into his. Don't be afraid to get big here and back yourself up with the tail of your lead rope and push him out onto the circle. As long as you are consistent when he tries to cut you off, soon he'll stop doing it. Once on the circle if your horse tries to drift into the center of the circle, you can project energy onto a body part (e.g., shoulders, rib cage, hips) followed up with the tail of your lead rope if necessary to get him back out onto the circle. Another common mistake is constantly asking your horse to move forward once he's on the circle. This is nagging your horse. Give your horse a release for doing what you asked him to do, relax and ask him to maintain his gait until you ask him differently. This exercise will help you learn to read your horse's body language and see/feel when he's going to break gait so you can ask before he breaks gait to keep the pace. If he breaks gait, ask him to step back up, then remember to release. So stop swinging that rope, stop clucking, just relax. This would be the same in the saddle if you keep a leg on to keep your horse moving forward; pretty soon your horse is dull to your leg cues. When asking for a step up in gait, be sure your horse has an open door to flow through. Your body language must be clear. When you and horse are communicating well all you'll need to increase your horse's speed is an open door. The mistake I see is stepping on the gas by swinging your rope at your horse's hindquarters, but you never released your foot off the brake (open door), so your horse will either rear up, buck or stop altogether because he is unsure of what you are asking him to do. Open the door so your horse has a place to put the extra speed/energy.

I am asking WindTalker to move out on the circle to my right.

I use the tail of my rope to help encourage WindTalker to move away from the pressure.

I continue to focus on the outside of WindTalker's right shoulder, using the tail of my lead rope to help apply pressure.

Now I start to bump WindTalker's nose with my right hand by pulling on the lead rope while I continue to use the tail of the lead rope to apply pressure to that outside shoulder.

Finally WindTalker begins to move out on the circle. Stay strong and clear in what you want and help your horse find the right answer. Apply pressure where you need.

If you horse gets too close to you, or cuts into the circle, then use your energy and the tail of your lead rope to push him back out on the circle. Aim your energy in the middle of the rib cage. You can also step into him, as I am doing here in addition to the tools mentioned above.

To bring your horse in for a stop, bring your hands to your belly button and back up (the only time you come off your pitcher's mound) until your horse is straight.

I keep backing up.

WindTalker is now straight, so I raise my hands to put up my energetic wall asking him to stop and not come into my space.

## Significance

Circling is NOT lunging. I will repeat that again, this exercise is not to lunge your horse into mindless circles going round and round and round. Circling establishes trust, leadership, respect and feel. This exercise will also help you determine your horse's mood for the day; build transition quality; move your horse's body on the arc of a circle by creating a bend in your horse; and you will know if your horse is stiff anywhere in his body. This is another great warm up exercise for your horse. Before you head out on a new trail, have your horse circle a lap or two in both directions to ensure he is focused on you and ready to head out.

# 11 FENCE POST

Stand with your back to the fence and your horse facing you, just like how you started with the Circling exercise. You will use your new circling cues to ask your horse to move on a half circle and parallel his body up against the fence (as if your horse was tied to you, the fence post). At first your horse is not going to get that close to the fence and you will need to use disengage the hindquarters cueing to help parallel his body to the fence. Go as far as you think your horse can manage and reward. Then build getting him closer and closer to the fence as his comprehension and acceptance increases. Reward your horse and pause for a moment, then ask your horse to go the opposite way and parallel up against the fence. One side of your horse will get closer to the fence than the other in the beginning. Just work both sides individually with baby steps until your horse is comfortable being close up against the fence.

My back is to the fence and I am getting ready to cue Qamar to go to my right.

I use the same cue, opening a door, as I did for the Circle exercise.

Qamar moves on a half circle to my right.

When Qamar's nose "hits" the fence (I have to cue his nose due to the low fence line, you don't need to do this with a taller fence line) I ask him to bend his body, and parallel up to the fence. He does this by moving his hindquarters over.

I help direct Qamar's hindquarters over with my body language and energy directed at his hindquarters just like in Disengage Hindquarters exercise.

We work step by step until Qamar is parallel to the fence by directing the hindquarters over.

Qamar is now parallel and I reward him for a job well done.

## Troubleshooting

Your horse is not automatically going to parallel his body up to the fence. You're going to need to guide him and convince him it is a safe thing to do. So work with your horse. Find out where your horse's comfort zone is and then gradually expand his comfort zone until he's parallel to the fence. Use your personal energy bubble and project your energy at the hindquarters to direct your horse's body parts until they line up with the fence. When you push your horse too far, he will push back against you/the pressure. Ask him to move away from the pressure to a spot by the fence where he was comfortable and then release him and reward him. The key here is to build over time. Note: if you step too far out away from the fence to direct the hindquarters, your horse will see an open door between you and the fence and want to go through that open door. You can block the door with your energy projection as well as by taking a physical step back to block the space. Use the skills and cues from all the previous exercises to help you direct your horse to success with this exercise.

WindTalker does not want to get close to the fence, so he is pushing backing into the pressure. I continue to direct his nose and drive his hindquarters (pressure with energy and the tail of the lead rope).

WindTalker got close to the fence, then moved away immediately. I am directing his shoulders closer to the fence, but he is resisting against the pressure.

WindTalker is really pushing against the pressure, so much that he rears up. This can happen when you push your horse too far too fast. He doesn't want to get close to the fence.

Again WindTalker is pushing back against the pressure. When your horse overreacts like this, ask him to go as close to the fence as possible, then reward him and repeat. Be careful not to push too hard too fast, as this will cause problems. Work in baby steps to build your horse's confidence with getting close to the fence.

After all that, WindTalker finally got to a spot where he could relax near the fence, and I am rewarding him for that.

## Significance

We never want our horses to pull back when being tied. This exercise teaches our horse that when he is tied and he needs to move his feet, he can move from side to side instead of pulling back. This is extremely helpful when your horse is frightened by something. He won't panic, he will just move from side to side. When horses get scared, they need to move their feet. Their natural instinct is to run and look later. In our human world they cannot run, so we direct them to move their feet in a more constructive way.

It's also important for your horse to feel comfortable being close to objects. You can teach your horse to allow you to mount from the fence, or a log, or a stump when a mounting block is not available. Your horse needs to be calm close to fences to be able to open and close gates. For safety reasons while riding, it's important your horse stays calm next to objects, trees, underbrush, etc., out on the trail.

# 12 BETWEEN THE FENCE

Start about 20 feet away from the fence with your back to the fence and your horse facing you (note: your horse will also be facing the fence). You will use your new circling cues to ask your horse to move on a half circle around you at first, then back and forth between you and the fence. Start with a large space and eventually you'll get closer and closer to the fence as your horse becomes more comfortable. Your horse will be moving in half circles....as soon as your horse's tail lines up with your chest, start to ask him to change directions. Gradually decrease the distance between you and the fence. The final product is your horse can calmly walk between you and the fence through a distance about the width of his body.

Using my Circling cues I ask WindTalker to move to my right.

WindTalker moves to my right and moves between me and the fence.

Continuing forward, as soon as his tail reaches my chest I will ask him to change directions.

Asking WindTalker to change directions.

And continue back through between me and the fence.

WindTalker comes through pretty calmly.

I ask WindTalker to stop, so I can reward him for a good job.

## Troubleshooting

You will know when your horse is uncomfortable in the tight space because he will rush to get through to the other side, or he may decide that going over you is an easier way to release the pressure. Stay at this distance until your horse will walk calmly through. Only then, and most likely on a different day, can you decrease the distance. This is a gradual progression to a tighter and tighter space for your horse to go through. Do not rush your horse through this exercise. Go at his pace. He will tell you when he's uncomfortable. Get to a point where he can be comfortable, reward and move on to something else. Then pick up the exercise again the next day.

If your horse wants to run over you to escape the pressure, you might want to increase the distance between you and the fence to see if he starts to relax more. If you have increased the distance a large amount where your horse should not feel any pressure, but he still wants to run you over, then you need to go back to circling and master that exercise where he stays out on the circle. If you have reached a distance where he stops trying to run you over, work at that distance for some time. Then very slowly and gradually decrease the distance to the fence. You will most likely need to spend more time at each distance helping your horse feel comfortable. Remember to go at his pace.

## Significance

Horses are claustrophobic by nature. In the wild they do not willingly go into small, tight spaces, but we ask horses to live in stalls and travel in horse trailers all the time. Even on trail rides, we can encounter tight spaces with underbrush, close trees, etc. It is safer for you and your horse to be able to navigate tight spaces with calmness. This exercise helps horses who have problems trailer loading. It also helps build trust with your horse. Your horse is asking you, is it ok to go through here? You are saying with trust that yes it is.

Final product, Qamar moves calmly between me and the fence about the width of his body.

# 13 KEYS TO SUCCESS

* Going at the pace your horse requires (patience).
* Timing your release to the moment your horse gives you the slightest effort toward the desired goal.
* Know the signs of horse comprehension:
    * Licking and chewing
    * Looking like he might fall asleep
    * A relaxed demeanor
    * Yawning
    * Closing of the eyes and eye rolling
    * Head/body shaking - like after a good roll in the dirt
    * Combination of any of the above
* Breaking down the exercise into baby steps.
* Standing your ground and asking your horse to move away from you, even when he pushes back against the pressure.
* Not to be afraid of your horse.
* Ending on a positive note for the day.

**Summary**

These exercises lay the foundation for you and your horse to be successful in any riding discipline you venture to explore together. Key elements in a relationship with your horse are trust, respect and leadership. All of these exercises establish you as the horse's leader, and help you gain and earn your horse's trust and respect.

# LZ Photography

**$45 per Hour**
Includes full disk with pictures

Reasonably priced pictures of you and your horse, in a setting of your choice. Bring a change of clothes for different effects.

**Contact me for more information at Info@LZHorsetraining.com
or give me a call
(H) 303-751-6206   (C) 303-562-4234**

Groups, Trail Rides, Farm Shots or Shows. Sales- and Stallion promotional flyers, Conformation pictures or other. Also Cats, Dogs and other animals available. You request...

# ABOUT THE AUTHOR

Kim and Night

Kim Baker, MS, RMT, ECT is the founder of KB Natural Horsemanship and the radio host of "The Kim Baker Show ~ the amazing connection between horses, animals and humans." Listen at www.kimbakershow.com

KB Natural Horsemanship is the most integrated horse and animal program available. Utilizing visualization, energy, breath and meditation methodologies, we are dedicated to educating horse owners about the simple things they can do to improve their horse's lives. The results are a deeper relationship with your horse, a stronger partnership, and ultimately more knowledge about yourself.

Kim Baker is an author, animal communicator, holistic healer, certified Reiki Master Teacher and Equine Craniosacral Therapist, equine consultant, riding lesson instructor and natural horse trainer. In her field Kim stands out because she works with the whole horse (mind, body, spirit) as an individual instead of a one size fits all approach. Kim also writes for local, national and international equine magazines and informational web sites. Kim's passion is helping horse and rider be the best they can be.

www.kbnaturalhorsemanship.com

Kim lives with her two dogs, two horses and a barn cat in Colorado.

**WANT TO SEE THESE EXERCISES IN ACTION?**

**DON'T MISS OUT!** Nearly 2 information-packed hours of **POWERFUL** information which will **TRANSFORM** your relationship with your horse to one you've only dreamed of!

Lead your bucking, rearing, disrespectful horse to the relationship you've always dreamed of!

*Echo was as wild as horses come. She would buck anyone or anything off! She also reared when she had a mind to. No one wanted her. She was passed from trainer to trainer with no improvement.*

*Finally one trainer took Echo on. With some dedication, patience, and following the 7 steps of "Groundwork Essentials," Echo turned into the DREAM HORSE for one young girl. The girl fell in love with Echo, and they rode off happily into the sunset.*

Hi, I'm Kim Baker, and I'm the trainer that helped Echo find her forever friend. And now, whether you have a bucking bronco, or are just trying to deepen the connection you and your horse know is waiting for you, I can help.

My DVD program, "Groundwork Essentials" is designed to show you:

* How to regain your horse's TRUST.

* How to earn your horse's RESPECT.

* How to create a wide open channel of COMMUNICATION between you and your horse.

* How to develop a DEEPER, RICHER CONNECTION with your horse.

* How to avoid common mistakes horse owner make that DESTROY their relationship with their horse.

* And much more...

## GET YOUR COPY TODAY!!!

**Only $34.97** (plus shipping and handling) *That's about what you'd pay for ONE meal out for a family of four!*

**GET IT HERE:** kbnaturalhorsemanship.com/shopping-corral

**STOP** BEING AFRAID OF YOUR HORSE AND LEARN HOW TO CREATE THE RELATIONSHIP AND PARTNERSHIP YOU'VE ALWAYS DREAMED OF!

*$1 FROM EVERY DVD GOES TO HAPPY DOG RANCH RESCUE 501C3 FOUNDATION TO SUPPORT ANIMALS IN NEED AND THAT PROVIDE THERAPY TO OTHERS.*

Made in the USA
Columbia, SC
27 October 2020